FOR YOU

Ian McEwan is the author of two collections of stories and eleven novels, including *Enduring Love*, *Amsterdam*, for which he won the Booker Prize in 1998, *Atonement*, *Saturday* and *On Chesil Beach*.

This libretto for Michael Berkeley's opera
was commissioned by Music Theatre Wales
and received its first performance on
May 31st 2008 at Theatr Brycheiniog.

IAN McEWAN

For You

The Libretto

VINTAGE BOOKS
London

Published by Vintage 2008

4 6 8 10 9 7 5

Copyright © Ian McEwan 2008

Ian McEwan has asserted his right under the Copyright,
Designs and Patents Act 1988 to be identified as the author
of this work

Vintage
Random House, 20 Vauxhall Bridge Road,
London SW1V 2SA

www.vintage-books.co.uk

Addresses for companies within The Random House Group Limited
can be found at: www.randomhouse.co.uk/offices.htm

The Random House Group Limited Reg. No. 954009

A CIP catalogue record for this book
is available from the British Library

ISBN 9780099526995

The Random House Group Limited supports The Forest
Stewardship Council (FSC), the leading international forest
certification organisation. All our titles that are printed on
Greenpeace approved FSC certified paper carry the FSC logo.
Our paper procurement policy can be found at
www.rbooks.co.uk/environment

Mixed Sources
Product group from well-managed
forests and other controlled sources
www.fsc.org Cert no. TT-COC-2139
© 1996 Forest Stewardship Council

Printed and bound in Great Britain by
CPI Bookmarque, Croydon, CR0 4TD

FOR YOU

Opera in two acts by Michael Berkeley
Libretto by Ian McEwan

World Premiere performed by Music Theatre Wales on
31 May 2008 at Theatr Brycheiniog, Brecon

Conductor   Michael Rafferty

Director   Michael McCarthy

Original Cast

Charles	Eric Roberts
Robin	Christopher Lemmings
Joan	Rachel Nicholls
Antonia	Helen Williams
Simon	Jeremy Huw Williams
Maria	Allison Cook

Act 1

SCENE ONE

Lights down. The discordant sounds of the orchestra warming up. Violins on open strings, sudden runs on brass, woodwind etc. Slowly, this tangle begins to organize itself.

*As it does so, **Charles Frieth** comes upstage, baton in hand, towards the orchestra. He is an eminent composer in his mid-sixties, now rehearsing one of his own early works.*

*From the shadows he is joined by his secretary, **Robin.***

*Lingering in the background is **Maria**, the Frieths' Polish house-keeper, an ungainly woman.*

Charles Don't tell me.
I know that look of yours.
How long do I have them?

Robin Only twenty minutes more. No longer,
or we have to pay them overtime.
Maestro, you know the rules are very strict.

Charles Damn your rules man.

Robin They are not my rules.

Charles I said damn your rules.

He raises his baton.

This has been a long morning.
I'm tired and unhappy.
My temper is beginning to fray.
Let us try again, from letter D,
the tutti marked piano ...

*He mops his brow with a towel and lets it fall into Maria's hands.
He conducts, the music finds its course.*

Tenderly ...
Sweetly ...
Now attack!

*Charles comes away, lost in thought, confiding while the music
continues.*

It does not touch me,
this music of my younger self,
when my name was unknown
and I lived on nothing but sex
and cigarettes and fast food,
when I was in love again every other week.
I hear it clearly, each intricate part,
I understand it, even admire it,
but I cannot feel its passion,
the longing, the sharp hunger,
the lust for newness of that young man.
It does not touch me now.

The car is ready, Sir!
The usual table, Maestro?
The Minister of Culture is waiting.
A famous man with a rich wife—but
the dimmed perception, the expiring powers,
stamina, boldness, vigour wilting
under the weight of years.
The long descent to uselessness.
Every man's fate, how banal it is,
and still it makes me angry, the clock
that's beating me to extinction.
Stop! Enough! How can I make it stop?

He has returned to the orchestra.

And stop and stop and stop!
God fucking damn, I called a halt.
Am I standing here for nothing, waving my arms?

Through this, the orchestra comes to a slow, untidy halt. Silence.

I am not entirely deaf or stupid.
There was a note, a wrong note, a broken note,
an F sharp that should have been a G,
a hot needle in my ear.
It was the French horn. You, yes you, my dear.

Joan stands, holding her instrument. Anxiously, Robin comes forward.

Robin Charles, she is a most promising player.

Charles You my dear. Yes, you.

Joan I did my best with what you wrote.

Robin Not this. Please God, not this again—

Charles Have you ever played that thing before?

Joan The note was high, almost beyond the instrument's range.

Robin Humiliation, then forgiveness, then seduction.

Charles Do you know which end to blow through?

Joan I'll try again. Please let me try again.

Trio

{**Robin**
{Charles, she is a most distinguished player.
{Not this. Please God, not this again—
{Humiliation, then forgiveness, then seduction.

{**Charles**
{You my dear. Yes, you.
{Have you ever played that thing before?
{Do you know which end to blow through?

{**Joan**
{I did my best with what you wrote.

{The note was high, almost beyond the instrument's range.
{I'll try again. Please let me try again.

*Joan leaves, distraught. Charles leaves separately. Robin remains
with the orchestra.*

SCENE TWO

The sitting room of the Frieths' London house. Charles's wife, Antonia, watches as Simon Browne, a surgeon, drink in hand, admires a wall of paintings.

Antonia It was kind of you to see me at home.

Simon I'm here as an old friend, not as your doctor.

Antonia I should be taking my turn in your waiting room.

Simon Another chance to see these beauties—
Ancher, Munther, O'Keeffe.
And you . . .

Antonia Yes, some say these women painters
were on the verge of greatness.
But Simon, look at me. I'm so full of fears.
Another operation. I cannot bear it.

Must it be so soon?
I need to ask you—is there no other way?

Simon A resection, and a biopsy to put our minds at rest.
A relatively simple procedure.
Trust me when I tell you, there is no other way,
and we must act now.

He pauses.

Is it your old fear that's haunting you?

Antonia Yes. It's ridiculous, I know.
My old fear,
the anaesthetic, the general anaesthetic.
The word 'general' sounds so sinister
to my ear.

Simon Perfectly safe these days. How many times
must we go through this?

Antonia I dread that moment of oblivion,
that rehearsal for death.
The cheerful porter with his trolley

coming to collect me from the ward.
I think of Charon, the boatman,
taking me across the River Styx.
Then corridors, fluorescent ceiling lights,
the elevator to a special little room,
the calming voices,
the cannula inserted, the chemical poison,
then coldness racing up my arm
with such violent speed,
and then, nothing, nothing.

Simon Exactly, nothing, and nothing to fear,
and when you wake . . .

Unnoticed, Maria comes in with a tray.

Antonia If I wake. What did the poet write of death?
The anaesthetic from which none comes round.

Simon Best not to think of Larkin at such times.

Antonia I know you think I'm a neurotic woman.

Simon I know you are an unhappy woman.

He pauses.

Where's Charles? Does he know?
I heard his concerto on the radio.
I don't pretend to like his music.
The notes seem plucked at random,
and what a din! A choir of tomcats!
But I'm a simple type who prefers Vivaldi.

Antonia He's working late.

Simon Again?

Antonia Working late again.
Working is the word we cling to,
Working is our household euphemism.
We live a privileged life of lies.

Simon *(softly)*
You must pack a case.
I'll come back for you tonight
if I can find a bed that's free.

He goes towards her, hesitates.

Too much to say.

Antonia Yes. Too much to say.

Simon Impossible to say it.

Antonia Impossible. And no need.

Simon Because you know.

Antonia We know.

Simon Only silence.

Antonia Silence will say it all.

Repeats, overlapping.
Simon takes his coat.

Simon I'm late. I must leave you. A doctor's duty.

Antonia The hospital? At this hour?

Simon A reception at the Garrick in honour
of a retiring surgeon. The glinting tray of canapés,
an indecent multitude of colleagues,
oily speeches of passionate insincerity.
I think we can all agree,
this is not an age of plain speaking.

Antonia, you must not worry,
it will work out well.

Antonia You must go.

As they turn, they notice Maria. Simon nods to her and leaves.

Antonia Maria. How long have you been standing there?

Maria I just came in this moment
with refreshments for your visitor.

Antonia I didn't hear you.

Maria The door was open, the doctor was just leaving.

She sets down the tray.

Will it be two for dinner tonight?

Antonia I shan't eat tonight. I'll be in my room,
and don't want to be disturbed.

Antonia leaves.

SCENE THREE

Maria Yes, I agree, a privileged life of lies,
But no one asks for my opinion—
Maria, who cooks his intimate
late-night suppers, who launders
the love-stains from his sheets,
removes the cup with its bloody
lipstick cicatrix, who sees it all,
the misery uncoiling because
in this house no one speaks.
Oh, the worthless, worthless women
he wastes his time on.

She complains, she whines about his
misdemeanours, the little crime she
longs to commit herself. But she prefers
virtuous hollow fidelity,
and sour long-suffering
so she can feel superior, and tragic,

while her illness is her only career.
She won't even kiss the good doctor
panting at her heels . . .
But she married the most exciting man
in the world. A lion among hyenas.
A genius, they say. I say, a god.
The room he enters fills with golden light.
It's the details that possess me—
the manly angle of his jaw,
the dark hairs curling on his wrist,
the pale hand that holds the baton,
the penetrating gaze of dark brown eyes,
a voice of warmth and power . . .
She married him, she has his name,
but she cannot keep him
from other women.

Ah, if only, if only . . .
I would give him what he wants—
I think I know.
Indeed I know his needs—
the little sensuous cruelty
he likes to inflict, and anal
and oral, and strange positions.

I'm more able than I look.
To drive all other women from his life!
Then all his music would be for me,
and I would make him joyous!
Delirious! Ecstatic!
Mine, and mine alone!

Robin enters.

Robin Oh, Maria, it's only you.
I wondered what the din was.
Be a sport and make some coffee.
I've had such an awful day with Charles.
What a piss-pot pompous fool he is,
a bully, a fraud, a mediocrity.
Oh God, I'm beginning
to sound like him myself.
A pot of coffee, and a cheese plate?

Furious silence

. . . with pickles?

Maria You know where the kitchen is.

I'm not paid to fetch and carry for you.
And don't leave a mess!

Robin Is everyone from Poland like you?

Maria In Poland we speak our minds.

Robin I always meant to visit,
but now you've put me off.

Maria relents and brings the tray to where he sits.

Maria

Song
Ah, Robin, you should go.
It's so beautiful and sad.
We have virgin forests
of the kind you lost in England
five hundred years ago,
where wolves and eagles hunt,
and clear rivers you can
put your lips to and drink.

Robin How romantic! I've heard the cities
are rather grim, and in between
are treeless potato fields.

Maria The conquering armies
from east and west forgot
to crush that lingering beauty,
though they almost crushed
our spirits. But now we are free
there's a newer sadness in our hearts.
The lovely town where I grew up,
is falling silent, becoming old.
We, the young, are fleeing west—
the plumbers, nurses, carpenters,
should be making a new Poland—
but money has lured us away.

Robin Don't blame money, blame yourselves.
If you really care about your hometown,
go back there, or stop complaining.

Charles *(offstage)* Robin! I need you.
Goddamnit man, where are you?

Robin Not again! Will I ever get a moment's peace!

Maria So resign, or stop complaining.

Enter Charles. Someone is with him, but we cannot quite see.

SCENE FOUR

Charles *(exultant, manuscript in his hand)* Ah! Robin,
the master of elusiveness!
Always hiding when I need you.
Tomorrow's rehearsal, the orchestral parts,
are they all done?

Robin I did them all last week.

Charles There's an insertion I need to make.
You'll have to work all night.
Thirty-two bars for solo horn ...
floating, tumbling, sweetly falling,
gently sustained by muted strings ...

Joan comes forward.

Robin *(aside)* A moment of pure beauty in bed—
an insertion he needed to make!

Joan So exciting!
We had our differences,
then we made it up in a flash.
Now we have a working relationship.

Charles And Maria, you dear, you wonderful woman,
without whom this house would fall apart,
we need champagne, and supper for two,
in the studio.

Maria Jugged hare or goulash?
Venison or bream?
Pommes purées or sautéed?
Beetroot in a crust of salt?
Figs in port with lavender ice cream?

Charles I don't care. Just bring it.
My Demonic Aubade, wild summation of all I know,
all I've ever felt, brought to new expression,
a new dawn in thirty-two bars.
Dear boy, history will count you privileged
to write out these parts.

Joan Not since Britten, not since Mozart,
did the horn have such a friend.

Robin To work till breakfast on my evening off—
I humbly thank you from the bottom
of my worthless heart.

Maria *(aside)* 'You dear, you wonderful woman,
without whom' . . . I'm in a dream,
I can hardly stand.

He's sending me a message over the head
of this ambitious tart.

Charles A player of such sensitivity
and skill, such a gentle touch.
I feel she understands me.

Robin Who can doubt she does.

Joan For you, I'll always give of my best.

Charles Maria, a word in private if you please.

Maria Oh my heart . . .

She follows him out.

Robin Humiliation, forgiveness, seduction
in a single afternoon—oh,
the predatory vigour of the newly old,
spending the last of their small change.

SCENE FIVE

Charles's study.

Charles How was Antonia today? Did she see anyone?
Did she go out? Was she unhappy?

Maria No more than usual.
She moped in that restless way of hers,
tried to read, tried to eat, watched the TV
for half an hour, drifted round the house.
But her spirits lifted
when her good friend came, the doctor.

Charles He came again?
Simon with the soft-eyed bedside manner.
Did he stay long?

Maria I don't like to say this,
It's not my business . . .

Charles But it's mine, so tell me—

Maria I tried not to notice, I don't like to spy.
They were standing close,
he took her hand, she gazed at him,
he talked about a bed . . .

Charles A bed? He talked about a bed?
By what strange logic
am I feeling sick?

Maria He likes her . . .

Charles Likes?

Maria He's fond . . .

Charles Fond? You mean . . .

Maria I mean he loves . . .

Charles He loves her!
Ah, the knowing medical touch.
And she . . .

Maria Is still young. She's lonely,
she thinks she's beautiful,
she thinks she's ill,
she's full of sorrows.

He gestures her away

Maria leaves

Charles Full of sorrows because
I neglect her for my work,
and for my . . . for my pursuits.
There's no justice in my anger,
but nor can I deny it.
Under my nose, in my house,
a man meddling with my wife
in the name of medicine!
I'll show him some double standards
with my fists! That smooth-faced bastard,
that cheat, that liar, that professional disgrace!

Am I going insane?
I know enough to know the blame is also mine.
'Still young', 'lonely', 'full of sorrow',
while the woman waiting through there
is my fifth this year, perhaps the sixth.
Reliable, loving Antonia,
this was always our arrangement.
But have I got the strength of will to stop?
I hate the doctor, and I hate myself.

Maria, I need you. Maria!
(Have I got the strength? I need someone
to shame me into keeping my word).

Maria enters

Maria, I've made an important decision.
Be my witness to this promise.
That girl you saw will be my last.
I make this promise now,
in front of you.

Maria You are making this promise to me?

29

Charles Yes, to you. You know me well.
I'm making this promise to you.
She is the last, I swear to you.
I'm counting on you
to hold me to my word.

Charles leaves.

Maria I could tell myself it's a dream,
a psychotic interlude, pure desire
warping my senses,
wish fulfilment running wild—
but I know what I know.
Like all men, he barely understands himself.
Now at last he realizes
what I've always known.
He's made his worthless promise,
And he's almost, almost almost mine.

SCENE SIX

Charles's studio. He and Joan are on a bed among a tangle of sheets—becalmed.

Joan They say an erection never lies.
But this is also eloquent,
when you shrink before my touch.

Charles I don't understand,
I just do not understand.

Joan You think I'm ugly, or too demanding.

Charles That's not it at all.
You're beautiful, and I love
your demands. Please don't get dressed.
This has never happened to me before.

Joan That's what men always say.
Perhaps you're too old?

31

Charles Don't say that. Don't get dressed.
Come and sit beside me here.
That's right. And kiss me, kiss me.
Now see. That's better.
I'll make it up to you, I promise.

They continue to embrace and kiss.

Joan Yes, that's better, Yes, I see.
I'm sorry for my angry words,
I love your kisses, and
I'm beginning to feel you now ...

Charles My darling, everything will be fine.
My appetite is as strong as ever ...

Maria bustles in, bearing a tray.

Maria For you ...
Beetroot baked in salt,
venison to follow,
Just as you requested ...

Charles This is kind of you, but ...

Maria Figs in port, a hearty wine,
perfect for a working dinner,
for busy musicians who never know
when to stop.

*She fusses round them, determined to separate them, plumping up
pillows, arranging a table for Charles and Joan to eat in bed. Before
they can protest, they are lying side by side, in front of their feast.*

Charles Maria, this is kind of you,
but you should have knocked.

Maria The tray was heavy and my hands
weren't free. Shall I open the wine?

She takes the bottle. A knock at the open door.

Charles Now who the hell is this?

Robin enters

Robin Ah, Maestro, you're busy. Never mind.
There's a problem with the score.
Four bars missing from the strings.

Charles Four bars missing? Don't talk rot!
For goodness sake, the violins repeat.
Are you blind? Can't you see the mark?

Robin There is no mark, and my eyes are good.

Antonia enters with suitcase, followed by Simon.

Charles My God! Now this. She's leaving me
for the doctor and his bed.

Antonia approaches.

Antonia We agreed you'd never bring your work home.
Is this the flute whose husband owns a bank,
or the harp with the autistic son,
or the cello with the house in Wales?

Joan None of these. I am the horn.

Antonia Of course. The horn of plenty.

Joan That's cheap.

Antonia No, my dear, it is you who are cheap.
Has he offered you yet your solo of thirty-two bars?
And promised a concerto?

Angrily, Joan gets out of bed.

Joan *(to Charles)* Is this how it goes?
Is this how it always goes?

Antonia You are but one variation on a theme.

Sextet
(Charles beseeching Antonia; Simon trying to draw her away; Robin addressing Simon; Joan furiously getting dressed; Maria aside.)

{**Charles**—I'm losing you, and I'm to blame.
{**Antonia**—Home and hospital—scenes of pain.
{**Robin**—Oh, the sorrow that follows the arrogance of fame.
{**Simon**—This is not an age for speaking plain.
{**Joan**—Offering thirty-two bars to a woman again!
{**Maria**—He's made his promise, I'm making my claim.

Tutti
Silence and deceit,
ambition and defeat,
love, music, loyalty, self-delusion—
these are the elements of deadly confusion.

End of Act One

Act 2

SCENE ONE

Hospital. Around Antonia's bed are leads, tubes, life-support machines. The steady rhythm of the heart monitor sets the pulse of her thoughts as she begins to stir.

Antonia *(half asleep)* She said nothing at all,
and waited for him to come back.

She wakes

Song
On the border of memory and dreaming
I saw a couple on a London bridge
in an early evening snowstorm.
Hand in hand, wild in love,
with plans and hilarious cries
they strolled to the other side.
And oh what care they gave each other,
such intensive care in bed.

His work, her money, their freedom—
with no idea how grown-up life
could uninvent their love.

Then at last the idea came
with a roar of delighted applause
and with loud praise, and giddy fame,
profiles, parties, open doors.
And he grew to the shape of a lion,
his musical ambition swelled,
while she shrank to the size
of a household mouse.
Travel, concerts, hotels,
women in far-off places—
the world grew noisier and sad.
His work wouldn't tolerate children—
the house was silent and cold.

And I said nothing at all,
and waited for you to come back.

Fade up a low spot to reveal Charles in a chair, in his overcoat.

Charles I remember that snowstorm on the bridge

when we crossed the river to my first concert
at the Festival Hall, and as we walked
we were singing from The Magic Flute,
Mann und Weib und Weib und Mann—
my God, how happy we were.

He goes to her bedside.

Antonia Your oboe concerto, so graceful and free—
you told me it was a love letter in music.
And when the crowds could let you go
we drank champagne on a riverside rooftop—
the city below us was silent and white.

Charles That terrace belonged to a millionaire
whose name is lost to me.

Antonia And we danced on the snow ...

Charles Drunk on music and love.

Sudden shift

Antonia *(aroused)* Then one month later, you fucked the oboist.

So began the endless succession—
what we kindly called your 'work'.

Charles Don't think of these things when you've
just come out of major surgery.

Antonia After such butchery, what better time?

Charles I can't ask you to forgive me for things I did
so wilfully. After all these years, one more apology
would be an insult.

Antonia *(subsiding)* For once you speak the truth.

Charles All I ask is your patience, give me
time to earn your trust, time to show you,
not in words but actions, that I have come back.
Let's cross another bridge together.

Antonia My limbs are heavy, I feel I'm sinking, but
by morphine's clear light I see it now.
I think you know there's a man who loves me.

Simon and a nurse enter, unobserved.

42

Your jealousy and pride have been provoked.
This is not sorrow, or a change of heart,
but blind possessiveness, the lifelong habit
you have of taking what you think is yours.

Charles *(rushes to her bedside)* Don't say that!
My darling, I want to show you how
I have changed. I've made my decision,
I've made a solemn promise ...

Accidentally, Charles knocks a monitoring machine to the floor.
Simon and the nurse rush forward to pull Charles away.

Simon Come away from those lines! What are you
thinking of? Are you trying to kill her?

Nurse Her life depends upon these machines.
You must not come so close.

The nurse tends to Antonia, who is falling asleep.

Charles We were just talking of treachery,
and I believe we were talking of you.

Simon *(moving Charles towards the door)* Leave her now.
She needs her rest. You should go.

Charles I have to speak to her. We need to be alone.

Nurse Please . . . please, no violence here!

Simon You need to be alone; she needs to sleep.
She's my patient, I know what's best for her.

Charles Yes, I've heard that's what you think.
Do you know there are ethical codes
for doctors and their patients?
And in my house,
there are rules of hospitality,
which you, my friend, have abused.

Simon And on my wards I have the final word.
I've asked you to leave. Shall I call security?

Charles *(furious, leaving)* A weak man hides behind authority—
It seems she's in your care. But listen doctor—
don't you dare exploit your position,
or I'll have you sacked. Whatever you say,
she's my wife and she belongs to me!

44

SCENE TWO

The Frieths' London house. Charles's studio. Maria is tidying up.
Robin sits at a table surrounded by music manuscript in piles. On
the floor, discarded balled-up sheets.

Robin Sixteen hours of writing out parts—
thirty-two bars for his latest squeeze,
then he wants to change the orchestration,
now he's unhappy with the strings—
I'm so tired these notes are swimming before
my eyes like drunken fish.
The rehearsal starts this afternoon.
My kingdom for a computer program—
but the old fool won't allow it.

Maria Count yourself lucky to be working for a genius.

Robin Aubade—a beautiful name for a poetic form—
the poet sweetly greeting the rising sun,

45

then parting sadly from his lover,
or tenderly begging her to stay.

But here comes 'Demonic Aubade'—
the great composer torments the dawn
with his fashionable racket. At his age
he should be thinking of the sunset.

Maria Pure jealousy. You want to be a composer—
I've seen the torn up pages in your filthy room.
But you know in your heart you have no talent.

Robin Does this mean that once again
you refuse to pour me a little cup of coffee?

Maria I've better things to do. This is
an important day, the important rehearsal
for his most important piece.
Destiny is calling him, history drives him forwards
and he needs my help. He's relying on me ...

Robin To iron his shirts—you poor deluded slave.

Enter Charles, straight from the hospital, still in his overcoat, still angry.

Charles Not finished? Have you been asleep?
How much longer are you going to be?

Robin I need another half an hour.

Charles I want you to go to the rehearsal rooms now—
make sure the percussion has been delivered.
It's urgent—remember the disaster we had last time.

Robin *(keeps writing)* How can I ever forget?

Maria relieves Charles of his coat.

Charles Clash and suspended cymbals, tam-tam, roto-tom,
timpani, bass drum, temple blocks,
mark tree, side drum, vibraphone—
make sure they're all in place.

Robin But they're waiting for these parts . . .

Charles When I say now it's now I mean—
you can finish when you return.
Don't sit there man, get going!

*Robin leaves. Charles paces restlessly. Maria pours him coffee
from a flask and waits.*

Duet
Truly, Maria
I'm surrounded by fools on this crucial day
when my mind should be clear . . .

Maria *(aside)* Oh my love, I could comfort him now.

Charles . . . clear of this anguish, this weight of sorrow.
If only I could live without a woman . . .

Maria *(aside)* He means without his wife.

Charles I should never have married her,
and tied myself up in lies.

Maria *(aside)* He dares not tell the truth about our love.

Charles How can I wipe away the past,
how can I persuade her that I love her?

Maria *(aside)* He's ashamed of his wretched marriage,
and now he must tell her that he loves me.

They come face to face. Maria offers the cup, he waves it away.

Was the operation a success?

Charles Oh yes, a success. Antonia will not die—
the good doctor has done his work,
but I could wring his neck, that loathsome snake.

Maria *(aside)* Angry with the doctor for saving her worthless life!

Charles If murder was among your household duties
I'd send you to the hospital now. Hah!

Maria *(aside)* To succeed where the doctor failed,
and end her misery!

Charles But I know that I'm a hypocrite and a fool . . .

Calmer now, Charles is picking up some manuscript papers. Half distracted, he glances at Robin's work as he starts to leave.

Let me put to you a simple question—
Maria, have you ever thought of marriage?

Maria You're asking me! Oh no, I mean, but yes, but no,
but yes, I mean, my answer is of course,
it's yes of course, a simple yes.

Charles I didn't mean to embarrass you. Just think
carefully, is all I have to say. Most carefully.
Not only of the hurt that's done to you—
be careful of the pain that you might cause.
Remember my example.

He leaves.

Maria But my love, I'll never cause you pain,
and I know you'll never hurt me.

Charles *(off)* Send Robin to me when he's back.

Maria picks up Charles's coat and hugs it to her.

Maria

Song
When I hear your voice I feel
the pangs of greedy craving.
I know you suffer as much at least—
we share the hunger before the feast.

You set the matter out so well—
the command concealed behind a laugh,
and then you put your question to me—
do you think I didn't answer clearly?

My life was as dull as housework,
days forgotten in repeated chores,
lifting, wiping, cleaning—
now at last my tasks have meaning.

Let me lift your weight of sorrow
undo the lies, wipe clean the past.
My household duty is obedience—
my answer dear is a loving yes.

But I must bind you to me
before you change your mind,
make of love a gorgeous cage
where you, my sweet, can gently age.

SCENE THREE

The hospital. Antonia in the ICU. The machines as before. The nurse and a junior doctor are tending the patient as Simon enters.

Junior Doctor All her signs are good. She's stable, but she's weak, her pulse is thready.

Nurse It's too soon to send her to the ward.

Simon Then we'll keep her here another day . . . before you go I want to tell you this: her husband is certain to come back, and when he does you must let me know at once. His state of mind is dangerous—

Nurse This morning when he went towards her bed I thought that he would kill her.

Junior Doctor The whole hospital is talking of it.
Hard to believe of such a famous man.

Simon Jealous fantasies, greed about her wealth,
the pressures of the creative life,
even a psychiatric disorder—
who knows—these may all be stupid stories,
but we'll take no chances—do not leave him
alone in here.

The nurse and junior doctor leave.

I cannot leave him alone with her—
but who will ever forgive this abuse
of professional power, or cure
my feverish sickness of deceit?

When I performed the tricky operation
I knew I was saving her for myself,
I've told no one of our connection,
that I've loved her and waited seven years.
Love has made me a specialist in fraud,
senior consultant in deception.
Now he wants to take her back, stake a

forceful claim to what he fears he'll lose.
He'll wheedle, threaten, repent, atone—
I dare not leave him alone with her.

Antonia *(stirring)* And waited for you to come back . . .

Simon Antonia . . .

Antonia He'll never change my mind.
I've told him. He knows . . .

Simon Yes, he knows, and he wants you back.

Antonia He cannot touch me now that I'm with you.

Simon With me—that's what I've longed to hear.
But Antonia, are you fully awake?
Do you know what you're saying?
Do you know where you are?

Antonia I'm drifting high above an endless plain
that's green to the curved horizon.
I'm moving towards you,
from misery to warmth,

from coldness to truth,
from silence to joy.

Simon No need for silence.

Antonia So much to say.

Simon Yes. So much to say.

Antonia And at last we can say it.

Simon The misery is over.

Antonia Because we know.

Simon We know.

Antonia Only joy.

Simon Joy will say it all.

*Repeats, overlapping. They kiss. Unseen by them, a dark figure
in a black coat moves downstage in low light.*

I'm needed in theatre.
I'll come back soon.

They kiss again.

Antonia I'll sleep now, my darling.
But come when you can.

Simon leaves.

Antonia *(falling asleep)* On the borders . . .
On the borders of dreaming and waking
I saw a couple . . .
I saw a couple falling in love . . .

Maria moves quietly upstage.

Maria What agony, to stand in the shadows
listening to this conniving pair—
her hateful pride dressed up as virtue
and he a compulsive liar
by his own confession.
How dare they call it love,
this cringing, timid, dishonest affair.

How can it measure against my own?

She goes towards the bed.

Only the rich sleep so deeply,
so sweetly unconcerned.

The final impediment to bliss.
My instructions were clear,
and I'm not strong enough
to resist the power of their logic

My household duty
is to uproot the weeds—

*She wrenches out leads from the life-support machines. Slowly,
deliberately, she lets Charles's coat slip from her shoulders to the floor.*

No one saw me arrive,
no one will see me leave.

Maria melts back into the shadows.

Antonia *(softly)* I'm cold, so cold,

The house grows silent and cold.
And I can say nothing at all
while I wait for you to come back,
while I wait for you, while I wait . . .

The monitor flatlines; the rising din of an orchestra tuning up.

SCENE FOUR

The rehearsal room. The tuning-up continues. The A is sounded and taken up. Charles comes upstage towards the orchestra, baton in hand. Robin is with him. Maria is to one side with a fresh towel for her master.

Charles Is all the percussion here?

Robin Every last item safely delivered.

Charles You've got rid of that horn player?—
I've forgotten her name.

Robin Yes, her replacement is that bearded fellow.

Charles takes up his position.

Charles Ladies, gentlemen,
I'm deeply honoured that your famous orchestra
will give the world premier of Demonic Aubade.

The orchestra applauds. Charles raises his baton, the piece begins
while he describes it.

A dust-reddened sun lifts itself
over the cold desert rim.
Soon we feel the harshness of the rays,
the searing white heat of creation
like the imagination
striving in its birth pangs.
Straining to give life.
This music too is a rising sun,
ever more fiery as it proceeds
until we must avert our gaze . . .

and find shelter. The sun becomes
the face of God at which we may not stare.

Charles comes away from the orchestra.

The light of artistic creation is also blinding.
The artist can't see the suffering he causes
to those around him. And they'll never
understand the purity of his goal, how the heat
of his invention won't melt
the ice in his heart.

He must be ruthless!
No religion, no purpose except this:
make something perfect before you die.
Life is short, art is for all time—
History will forgive my ways because
My music outstared the sun.

Enter unobserved a plainclothes police woman, Detective Inspector Black; a uniformed woman police constable, WPC White; and Simon, distraught. WPC White holds over her arm Charles's coat.

Charles returns to the orchestra as the Aubade reaches its climax.

Charles It lifts! It soars!

DI Black Is he the one?

Simon This is the man. This is her husband.

White, Black If you don't mind, sir.

Charles Nothing can withstand its power!

White, Black We'd like a word.

Charles Its fury and its heat!

White, Black This won't take long.

The orchestra comes to a ragged halt.

Charles How dare you intrude like this!

DI Black They told us we would find you here.

WPC White Is this yours?

Charles You've found my coat. How awfully kind.
Give it to my man, then, ladies, kindly leave.

White, Black We have some questions for you.

The exchange becomes fast and stormy.

Charles Questions? Questions? Questions?
Do you realize where you are, and who I am?

WPC White Did you leave it at the bedside
of your dying wife?

White, Black, Simon This coat you say is yours!

Charles Dying? Did you say dying?

DI Black You left in a hurry. Were you disturbed?

Black, White, Simon You ran for your life!

Charles Dying? I don't understand.

Simon Did you kill her because it was me she loved?

White, Black, Simon Your jealous frenzy!

WPC White Was it her money you wanted?

White, Black, Simon Your vicious greed!

DI Black A nurse and doctor saw you make
a failed attempt upon her life.

White, Black, Simon You can't deny it!

Robin Surely there's been a misunderstanding.
Why don't you sit down.

Maria *(aside)* Every minute brings him closer to me.

Charles Am I going mad?
What is this talk of killing and dying?
How can I answer your questions
when my wife is not dead?

Simon What odious pretence of ignorance!

DI Black *(as WPC White applies handcuffs)*
Not dead! A good defence.
You can put it to the judge.

WPC White Not dead—a matter of opinion, perhaps!
Hah hah! This way, my friend.

She begins to lead him away.

Charles *(softly beseeching)* Please tell me Antonia is not dead.

DI Black You'll find no one who can tell you
she was not murdered in her hospital bed.

Charles Murdered . . .
Who could murder sweet Antonia?

He has come face to face with Maria.

No . . . no . . .

Maria remains silent.

But why?

WPC White This way now sir. Our car is waiting for you.

Maria For you, my sweet. For you.

White and Black begin to lead Charles away.

Charles Maria! You must tell them the truth!

Maria The truth is this. I know you better
than you know yourself. I know your
prison years will teach you how to love.
I'll make your cage a happy one.
In the desert of empty time, my visits
will be your sweet oases.

Charles Are you completely mad?
Tell them the truth!

Maria Like heroes in a prison movie, we'll
press our hands together against
the thickened glass.

Charles This is the killer. Arrest her!

White, Black This way now.

Maria And when at last they set you free,
and you are old and frail
I'll take you home with me
and care for you, and care for you.

Charles I am not the killer. Please listen to me!

White, Black, Simon, Robin, Maria
The lonely years in your happy cage,
the sweet oasis of her (my) visit.

Maria This is the gift I brought—

White, Black, Simon, Robin, Maria For you!

Charles I am . . .

Maria I am the only lover.

White, Black, Simon, Robin, Maria For you!

Charles I am already . . .

Maria And I will wait—

White, Black, Simon, Robin, Maria For you!

Charles I am already in hell.

White, Black, Simon, Robin, Maria She (I) will wait for you.

Charles is led away.

Maria remains.

Ends

www.vintage-books.co.uk